Mysterious Ways

A Memoir of Spiritual Awakening and Healing

Edward V. Tuttle

BOOKS BY EDWARD V. TUTTLE

Sacred Stories Sacred Dreams:
Bible Myth and Metaphor

Raindrops in the Dust:
Dreams, Memories and Reflections

Mysterious

Ways

A Memoir of Spiritual Awakening and Healing

By

Edward V. Tuttle

Pathways of Light

Santa Maria, California

LCCN 2007922791

ISBN 0-9716484-7-6

Pathways of Light
P. O. Box 1123
Santa Maria, CA 93456

Cover design: Alpha Advertising

Preface

Mysterious Ways traces the course of one man's stumbling toward the light, and the life-changing experiences that led ultimately to an unshakeable faith in God's power and presence in our life. It is also a testimony to the incredible importance one's mind plays in the outcome of any event, particularly in the healing process.

The writer shares the story in the sincere hope that in God's own time and wisdom it will come to rest in the hands of those who find within its pages signposts to their own spiritual awakening and — healing. If it touches only one life in this way, it is enough.

1

Hoisting a chilled mug of Millers I said, "Here's to us babe; it's finally coming together." A happy grin on her face, Barbara raised her glass and we both laughed when Bryan, our three-year-old raised his Coke in imitation. In the mood to celebrate our new home we sat at a polished table in the Pizza Hut, breathing in the tantalizing aroma of fresh-baked pizza.

With a beautiful family and a future stretching out before me that promised ever more of this world's treasures, I was flush with success; my self confidence soared. I felt justifiably proud of what I had achieved in the six short years since moving to California from New Jersey, and was blissfully unconscious of the scriptural warning that *"Pride goes before destruction and a haughty spirit before a fall."*

Filled with pizza and soft drink, we left the air-conditioned interior of the restaurant and stepped into the welcome warmth of the afternoon sun. It was a picture postcard kind of California day; a light breeze blew in from the west under a cloudless blue sky to lay its soft touch on the quiet town of Thousand Oaks. I held my young son's hand as we walked to our new Cadillac De Ville, Barbara at my side.

As I reached to open the car door, the colorful pennants flying in front of the motorcycle dealership across the street caught my eye. "Mind if we stop over there for a minute?" I asked Barbara, as I lifted Bryan into the car.

"No, go ahead," she said.

I drove across the street and parked next to a line of sleek motorcycles, their vibrant paint jobs gleaming in the sun. I got out and walked over next to a Yamaha 650 XS, swung my leg over the machine and settled into the saddle. I took hold of the handlebars, with the feeling that this bike had been built just for me.

The owner of the shop approached, "Beautiful machine isn't it?"

"It is that."

"You ride?"

"Yeah."

"Take it for a spin," he said, handing me the key.

"Just like that?" I asked.

With a grin he pointed to our car. "I have your wife and son as security. You'll be back."

Looking over to where Barbara sat, with Bryan on her lap, I pantomimed taking the bike for a ride. She responded with an answering wave that said, "Go for it!"

Putting on a helmet, I punched the starter button. The engine came to life with a throaty growl. It spoke to me in a different voice than the `Harley Davidsons I had learned to ride in the State Police; softer, but no less powerful.

I lifted the kick stand into place with my heel, worked the clutch, shifted the bike into first gear and, with a gentle twist on the throttle, peeled out.

Traveling south on Thousand Oaks Boulevard, past the car dealers, I turned onto a black-top road that snaked its way back into the foothills.

The bike was magnificent, smooth and powerful; like a high-strung thoroughbred it responded to my lightest touch. I continued for more than a mile then, spotting a suitable place I swung an easy U-turn and headed back. As I approached a blind curve on the narrow road, my concern for on-coming traffic made me hug the right shoulder. The rear wheel struck a patch of loose gravel, the bike fish-tailed and, before I could regain control, slammed into a tree and I blacked out.

I awoke briefly and realized I was lying in the middle of the road. Removing my helmet, I tried to get up, but my legs folded under me and the blackness returned

... I glimpsed the faces of two young women ... and then nothing ...

... In another brief moment of consciousness I was aware of being in an ambulance racing down Thousand Oaks Boulevard, its siren screaming ... and again slipped into the void ...

Then, under the searing lights of the Emergency Room, in yet another moment of consciousness I heard a voice laced with concern ... *"His blood pressure is dropping."*

Stunned by the words, I realized for the first time how seriously injured I was and thought, *Son-of-bitch, I could die ... I could die right here.*

***

My first close-up look at death came ten thousand miles from home on an obscure island lost in the vastness of the Pacific — Peleliu. It is an insignificant outcropping of coral, northeast of the Philippines, measuring ten square miles, where more than sixty years ago men fought like primal beasts over its possession. In the space of ninety days the blood of more than twenty thousand dead and wounded was spilled on those few square miles of now-forgotten real estate. It was there I saw death up close and personal, brutal and unforgettable. I was nineteen — and a proud Marine.

It was there that I first asked the question — "Who or what is it that marks one for death and another for life?" It seems sometimes as though there is a gigantic crap game being played among the gods with the outcome resting on the throw of the dice from some celestial hand, and we ask — "Why?" We feel that it has to somehow make sense. It doesn't! But the question, like a recurring bad dream, haunts the mind of anyone who has ever been in combat and survived; "How is it that I lived and my buddies died?"

I was in the third wave of the assault, with a full pack on my back and a seventy pound radio, the size of a microwave oven, strapped to my chest. We stood grouped in the belly of an amphibious tractor as it plowed its torturous way over the reefs toward shore, while we saw others like it blown out of the water by Japanese artillery firing from the ridges. It reminded me of the line of little white ducks that creep across the back of a carnival shooting gallery. We were sitting ducks!

It appeared we were lucky, we missed being blown out of the water, and the beast that carried us in its belly finally shuddered to a stop a few yards short of the beach. It opened its mouth as the landing ramp was lowered and disgorged us into surf up to our waist.

I struggled against the sucking drag of the wet sand and water and finally made it to the beach — a bloody brutal beach already littered with the bodies of comrades. Someone shouted, "Get down you dumb bastard, they're right there!" And I really hit the beach.

The blistering sand, the cries of wounded, the constant artillery and small arms fire all fused together to create a living hell on earth. The blood-red scorching sun finally surrendered to the Pacific and darkness descended on the first day.

By nightfall we had gained a few hundred yards and our initial objective, a small airstrip. We hunkered down. Exhausted, I dug a shallow foxhole in the sand, and waited and watched. The darkness was shattered by the intermittent flash and blast of incoming artillery rounds, and the return fire from our ships off shore. The ground trembled under the pounding — and I with it.

Death stalked the earth indiscriminately in a deadly rain of high explosive. It was there I first looked death, the distinct possibility of my death, right in the face. It's true that the Marines turns boys into men, but nothing in the training can prepare anyone for that moment, for the crystal-clear realization — I could die here. At any moment, I could die.

By morning of the second day a great deadening calm came over me when I decided I was either going to live, or I was going to die, and I didn't have a whole lot to say about which was to happen. In that moment my mind, my very soul, was etched deeply in some irrevocable way by that stark, brutal, truth. A cold shield settled around my heart.

In the days that followed, I went about my duties shielded by that coldness, cloaked in it — a stone where my heart had been. There was no sense of worry about living or dying, each day had its duties and one day followed another ... and another. On the surface there was no change but, deep within, the warrior was born.

I survived.

2

I awoke lying flat on my back in a soft bed, thirsty but feeling no pain. An intravenous drip hung on a stand next to my bed, and a monitor somewhere behind me emitted a slow, steady beep that I recognized as my heartbeat.

A nurse stood at my bedside. "Ah! You're awake. How do you feel, any pain?"

My throat so dry I could only croak, "No. Water please."

"Not yet, but you can have some ice chips. Would you like that?"

I nodded and opened my mouth. They melted on my tongue, cool and incredibly soothing. I must have died and gone to heaven and she was an angel.

She placed the call button next to my hand and said, "We're right here. Just press the button if you need anything."

I took a deep breath; I was alive!

I slept.

When I awoke, Barbara stood next to my bed. She held one of my hands between both of hers. "Welcome back," she said and gave my hand a squeeze.

"Honey," I said, "I don't think I'll buy that bike."

That brought a brief smile, but could not conceal the concern reflected in her eyes.

"Are you feeling much pain?"

"No."

"You really did a number on yourself," she said. "The doctors told me that your pelvis was split open like a book and you have a compound fracture of your lower left leg."

Her comment jogged my memory. "I remember trying to get up when I lay in the middle of the road. No wonder I couldn't."

"You lost a lot of blood; you were lucky they got you here in time. They ran short of your blood-type and the highway patrol made runs from all over the state to get enough. You had a lot of people working and praying for you."

A lump filled my throat, I couldn't speak. Fully aware now that my life hung in the balance, I was overcome with gratitude for all those who had acted to save it.

Tears filled her eyes. "They told me they didn't think you were going to make it, I guess to prepare me for the worst. I told them, 'You don't know this man''.

Still holding my hand between hers like a life-line through which she poured her strength, she leaned over and kissed me lightly on the lips. The stark realty that I could have died out there on that lonely stretch of blacktop hit me now with a force that took my breath away.

Swept up in a rush of emotion I clung to her hand like a drowning man to a life-preserver.

When she released my hand, she reached into her bag and withdrew a familiar object. Placing it in my hands she said, "I thought you might want this."

It was my Bible, the same one that Rev. Frank Huff had given me so many years before. The familiar feel of the soft black leather cover was like the touch of an old friend, comforting, reassuring. I placed it on my chest, over my heart. Overwhelmed, I could only nod my thanks.

She kissed me again and whispered, "I'll be back soon. Get some rest."

I closed my eyes and listened to her departing footsteps, my thoughts drifting back to those days when the Bible first came alive in my hands, and in my life.

***

The year was 1962, and I was in the throes of re-inventing myself after resigning from the State Police in 1960. I possessed a private investigator's license and was owner and director of the Bureau of Special Investigations, 10 Park Place, Morristown, New Jersey. I was my own boss with all the benefits and pitfalls that implies, but had managed my first year in business to double what I had earned my last year as a Detective Sergeant.

Cop or ex-cop, some things don't change. I had stopped for a cup of coffee at the Diner in

Boonton, my home town. There was an open stool at the counter next to Rev. Frank Huff.

He was a man in his mid-fifties, short and stocky, with gray hair and eyes, and a tightly trimmed military mustache to match. He wore a dark gray sport coat over a soft white linen shirt, and sported a bow tie that picked up the colors of both. He was by nature a quiet man; the bow tie was subtle evidence of an independent spirit.

Pastor of the First Reformed Church he had performed the ceremony when I married my first wife, Eleanore. We exchanged greetings as the counterman, without asking, placed a white mug of steaming black coffee in front of me. I ordered a slice of apple pie.

My wife and I were not regular church goers, so it came as a surprise when he turned to me and asked, "Ed, I have been wondering if Eleanore would be willing to teach a Sunday school class."

"I don't know," I replied. "You would have to ask her." I was surprised even more when I heard myself say, "But I'd be interested."

It was his turn to be astonished, an ex-cop, private eye, teaching Sunday school.

"Why that would be wonderful!" he stammered, "and I have just the class for you, a group of boys ages fourteen to twenty. They have just begun to read and discuss the book of Philippians."

The name sounded vaguely familiar but then my knowledge of the Bible could have been written on the head of a pin with room left over for the collected

16

works of Shakespeare. This was no time to confess my ignorance; I asked if there was a lesson plan.

"No," he said, "but these young fellows will keep you busy with questions. They're a bright and curious lot." With that he stood up, reached out and took my hand, "I really appreciate this, Ed. Sunday school is at 10:00, come a bit early so I can introduce you to the rest of the staff and the children."

We shook hands and he left, with me wondering what I had gotten myself into. The closest I had ever come to a spiritual discipline was The Power of Positive Thinking, by Rev. Norman Vincent Peale. That I had practiced with some success.

It was Tuesday; I had four days to prepare. I discovered the book of Philippians was not really a book but a five-page letter from the Apostle Paul to the people of the church at Philippi. Like all good stories it was set in high drama, for Paul wrote it from prison, uncertain whether he was to live or die.

I liked his no-nonsense approach when he wrote, "Work out your own salvation with fear and trembling; for God is at work in you, both to will and to work for his good pleasure."

And when he summed the letter up with these words: "Finally, brethren, whatever is true, whatever is honorable, whatever is just, whatever is pure, whatever is lovely, whatever is gracious, if there is any excellence, if there is anything worthy of praise, think about these things and the God of peace will be with you," I felt ready.

We sat in a circle in the choir loft, an assembly of shiny-faced, bright-eyed young men and myself, and shared our thoughts and questions. I made certain the quiet ones were heard, as well as those eager to display their ideas. In the process I learned far more than the boys; about Paul, about life, about myself. It was grand!

I felt a special joy, a deep sense of fulfillment, preparing for the classes, and began to appreciate what a practical book for living I held in my hands. It wasn't long before I brought my own version of Bible-based positive thinking to the full Sunday school assembly. Months passed and when the Sunday school superintendent had to make a career move out of the area, Rev. Frank asked me to fill the position.

"I'd like you to seriously consider it, Ed," he said. "Everyone likes you. You would be perfect for the job."

"I don't know about that, Reverend. I have too many questions and conflicting notions about the orthodox teachings of the church."

A smile touched his lips. "No better place for you to be, then," he replied.

With that I agreed, and in a brief Sunday ceremony accepted the post and was given a Bible signed by both the Superintendent and Rev. Huff.

***

That Bible now rested on my chest, large chunks of it embedded in my mind and heart. Preparing for those classes so many years ago opened my mind to its rock-solid wisdom and my heart to the beauty and power contained within its pages.

I closed my eyes, savoring the memory. When I opened them again there was a man dressed in a business suit standing next to my bed. He looked intently at me for a long moment, then picked up my Bible and sifted through the pages until he found what he was seeking. He studied it briefly then, without a word, he closed it and gently placed it back on my chest.

He moved to the foot of my bed and lifted the blankets exposing my feet. Taking a pen from his pocket he pressed the point against my right foot. "Feel that?"

I nodded, "Yes."

He moved to my left leg where only my toes protruded from the cast on my leg and again pressed the pen's point against my bare toes. ""How about that, feel that?"

"I do," I replied.

"Can you move your toes?"

I moved my toes, first the right foot and then the left.

"Very good ... very good, indeed," he said softly, and with a parting glance at my Bible still resting on my chest, turned and left.

I asked the nurse who he was and she said that he was their Chief of Staff and that he had been the lead surgeon on the team who had worked for hours to patch me back together. "He's the best," she said. "You were lucky that he was in the hospital Sunday afternoon when they brought you in."

Curious, I lifted the blankets and looked the length of my body. There was a cast on my left leg from my toes to the top of my thigh, and a spread to my hip bones that didn't look right — they were too wide apart. My pelvis lay spread outward like the broken wings of a bird lying on its back. The entire area felt like a bowl of jelly.

I lay my head back and pulled the blankets up under my chin. A heart-shaped Valentine hung open on a ribbon over my bed, placed there by some unknown angel. Written in bold script was, *"God is Love!"*

3

It was morning of the third day, February 9, 1971, when I heard the crash of glass and a frightened scream. The hospital rocked and swayed as though shaken by the hand of some playful giant. An earthquake!

My heart raced like a runaway engine, the adrenaline rush of fear instantaneous. Unable to move I absurdly wondered what floor I was on should the building collapse. But earthquakes only last for a few moments and soon everything stopped swaying and shaking and settled back into place. The quiet routine of the hospital returned and my heart resumed its regular beat.

I picked up my Bible and it fell open to Psalm 18, one I had never read before. Words and phrases leaped off the page, astonishing, unforgettable:

The cords of death encompassed me
The snares of death confronted me.
In my distress I called upon the Lord.
To my God I cried for help.
From his temple he heard my voice,
My cry reached his ears.
Then the earth reeled and rocked,
The foundations of the mountains
Trembled and quaked.

He reached from on high ...
He brought me forth into a broad place.
He delivered me.
He girded me with strength
and made my way safe.

The synchronicity of it took my breath away. The earth had indeed rocked, reeled, and quaked, and it was *I* who was being lifted, and girded with strength, and my way made safe. I took the words as a personal message, a promise "*Egocentric,*" a part of me whispered, "*You read too much into the coincidence.*" "*I think not,*" my soul responded," *God works in mysterious ways His wonders to perform.*" Nothing and no one could shake my full acceptance of the message, nor my wonder and elation at the unique manner in which it reached my eyes and my heart. I had not the slightest doubt; I *was* being lifted and girded with strength, and my way made safe.

It had not always been that way, I thought, as I remembered the day ... that terribly sad day when I cursed God.

***

My association with Rev. Huff and the Sunday school at the First Reformed Church lasted for nearly two years. It was a joyful time of sharing and growth as my understanding and appreciation of the Bible expanded, but it turned to ashes in my mouth one Sunday morning in September 1964, when my mother called to say that my brother Homer, and my sister-in-law Jean, had been in an accident and were in Riverside Hospital.

"Mom, are they alright?"

"Homer's hurt but he's okay," she sobbed.

"And, Jeanie? What about Jeanie?"

Now she was crying so hard she could not catch her breath.

"Mom! How's Jeanie?"

"Ah … son … she died," she gasped, now sobbing uncontrollably.

"No! Oh no, not Jeanie," I cried. I couldn't believe it!

Images of Jeanie filled my mind; an irrepressible, freckle-faced child of a woman, the mother of five small sons. Those boys, the youngest only eight months old, left without a mother. God! It can't be! God!

My heart felt like it was being torn from my chest. Filled with grief and a mounting rage I stumbled outside, stood under the open sky and, shaking my fist at the heavens; I screamed,

"Fuck you! If that's the kind of God you are, then fuck you!"

In that instant, whatever sense of God I had come to accept was utterly blown away. The feeling of loss and betrayal left in its wake a great emptiness; it was as though a black hole had opened up within me and swallowed every sense of God I had ever given thought to.

Ours was a tight-knit family; we lived next door to Homer and Jean, while our parents and my other brother and his wife, lived across the street. We were there for each other; we would survive and in time heal. But what was I to do with that empty space where God had been?

Nature abhors a vacuum, and my heart and mind did as well. With the passing days I felt the reawakening of a fierce desire for self-reliance and independence — even from God. I would be my own man, chart my own course in life, religion be damned.

I turned to the words and works of Ayn Rand, an avowed atheist and the founder of a philosophy of life called "Objectivism." It was a discipline built on the concept of rugged individualism where one's rational mind was the highest quality of man. It was founded on the principle that "man is an end in himself, not a means to the ends of others and, that man should think and judge independently, valuing nothing higher than the sovereignty of his own mind." (The Objectivist Newsletter, April 1962.)

I first met Ayn Rand in the pages of her book Atlas Shrugged and, though a work of fiction, the story opened my eyes and my mind to a view of my life that I had not previously recognized. The protagonist, Hank Reardon, was prisoner to his own misconceived idea of who, and what, he should be in the world rather than what his own mind told him he was meant to be. I was stunned when I saw a mirror image of myself in the character. It moved me to look at my life with fresh eyes and I didn't like what I saw.

I decided from that moment on I would trust the result of my own thought process and accept responsibility for the outcome. If my choices turned out poorly, I would know who to blame and where to look to make changes. Accepting full responsibility for my life whatever the outcome filled me with an incredible sense of freedom and power. The "iron string" of self-reliance that Emerson wrote about rang within me like a bell — and I thrilled to the sound of it.

I read every book she wrote, attended her lectures in Manhattan, and learned to think — really think — with a fresh clarity of mind, and purpose. The experience left an indelible imprint on my character and my life.

4

My day brightened when I saw my best friend Neil Aiken standing next to my bed. He grinned like a kid when he told me he had gained entrance by telling the nurses that he was my brother. He was my motorcycling buddy, and together we had explored a host of dirt roads and trails strung through the back-country.

On one of those jaunts his bike skidded out and Neil slipped over the edge of a dirt trail. He and his bike came to a rest against a skinny sapling growing out of the bank, just below the edge. It was the only thing that prevented him from plunging to the bottom of a deep ravine. I held my breath as I watched his cigarettes fall from his shirt pocket and drop toward the bottom of the gorge.

Luckily, he lay close enough to the edge of the trail that I could reach him. Lying in the dirt I grasped his hand and pulled him to safety, and together we got his bike back on the trail. He wasn't hurt, but he was in no mood to joke when he realized that it could have been him instead of his cigarettes lying at the bottom of the ravine. Laughing with relief we saddled up and continued our ride.

He looked at me now and shook his head. His eyes said it all. We both knew it could have been him lying in the bed.

We attended the same Religious Science church in Thousand Oaks; it was where we first met. We were barely acquainted when we had a discussion of which was better; to *know* or to *believe*. I forget which one I chose, I only remember we had a lively discourse and became fast friends.

He told me that he and his family and the whole church had me in their prayers. I took his hand in both of mine and gave it a squeeze. He turned away but not quickly enough to hide the tears in his eyes. With his back still toward me, he gave a wave and said, "I'll see you later, buddy."

I gave him a thumbs-up, which he didn't see, and said, "I'll be here."

I lay quietly thinking about how important a personal relationship with God had become in my life. The crystal-clear quality of Ayn Rand's philosophy had stimulated and satisfied my mind, but not my heart. In my heart there was a huge black hole, an emptiness where God had been, a barrenness I had pushed to the back of my mind. It surfaced in a most surprising way while I was on an exploratory trip to California in February, 1965.

* * *

Intent on changing my life I flew to San Francisco, rented a car, and traveled down the coast with the idea of finding employment and relocating. My plan was to contact fellow graduates of the FBI National Academy for leads. My first stop was in the beautiful coastal town of Santa Cruz where I had a pleasant, but fruitless, talk with the Chief of Police.

I left Santa Cruz behind and picked up state route 17, over the coastal range, for a connection with highway 101 in San Jose. As I neared the crest of the mountain I noticed a small, wood-framed chapel off to my right, its steep-pitched roof reaching toward the heavens. On an impulse I pulled into the empty, gravel-covered parking area, and turned off the engine.

I sat for some moments contemplating the simple elegance of the wayside chapel. Tiny though it was, dwarfed by the majestic evergreen-clad mountain rising behind it, it conveyed a statement of faith and endurance that welcomed the weary, perhaps lost, traveler.

In the grip of an unexplainable pull, I stepped from the car and walked up onto the small porch and tried the door. It was open! I stepped inside and stopped in amazement and delight; the sanctuary was flooded with light pouring through the back wall which was glass from floor to rooftop.

Instead of finding myself in a small enclosed chapel, spread before me was a glorious vision of earth and sky that seemed primal in its power and *beauty. Thick, stately stands of spruce and pine reached from deep within a gorge, the bottom of which was hidden behind a carpet of morning fog, and stretched their limbs up into a sun-drenched sky of startling blue. All of it so close I felt drawn into it, one with it.*

In that instant I was struck with the realization that my professed atheism of recent time was no more substantial than the morning fog that disappeared in the rays of the sun. I knew in that moment how much I had missed a personal relationship with my God, how vital it was to my life.

I sat wrapped in it, unaware of the passing hours, until I became conscious of the changing of the light. I offered up a quiet, heartfelt, prayer of thanks and left, closing the door quietly behind me.

I continued my trip down the coast and in Los Angeles was offered a position with security consulting firm owned by a former FBI agent and a retired LAPD sergeant. They promised to hold the position for me for a few weeks, while I settled my affairs in New Jersey.

In less than two weeks of my return home I found a buyer for my private detective agency, packed my 1965 Chevrolet convertible, picked up Barbara, and headed west.

It was early March when we arrived in the City of the Angels and found an apartment in North Hollywood, within an easy drive to the firm's downtown office. I began work the following day.

I was a quick study and soon learned a good deal about industrial security as I inspected facilities scattered throughout California and bordering states. But the novelty of it soon wore off, leaving in its wake a mind-numbing repetition to the work. After nearly a year, I asked for a raise. They refused, and I quit.

Considering that we lived in the middle of a city of fourteen million people, surely I could find more satisfying work, with better pay — I thought.

5

Barbara arrived soon after Neil left, I chuckled as I told her how he had conned his way into ICU to see me.

Not laughing, she said, "I passed him on the way in. He didn't stop, looked like he'd been crying. He's taking this hard."

"Yes, I know. He tried to hide it but I saw tears in his eyes as he left."

"Speaking of hard," I said, "that was one scary earthquake we had this morning; was there any damage at home?"

"No, we were lucky! It was centered in Northridge, near the hospital. It was damaged, and some freeway overpasses collapsed, but considering the severity of the quake there were very few dead. We can all be grateful for that."

"That's for sure," I said, and added, "This hospital swayed like a tree in the wind. I wondered what floor I was on, as though that made a difference if it collapsed."

"Well, I'm sure glad it didn't. You have had enough banging around for a while. Are you okay?"

"Yes, I am. You might say I got the word straight from the mouth of God," and told her about opening my Bible at random to Psalm 18 following the earthquake.

"I swear, it was as though God had spoken the words directly to me — a promise. The synchronicity was astonishing."

For the longest time she just looked at me, her eyes brimming with tears, then softly she said, "It doesn't surprise me, with all the people praying for you, and not just from our church."

"That's awesome! Thank them for me, and tell them to keep up the good work."

"I will," she said. Then kissing me lightly on the lips, she murmured, "You need to rest." And she left.

I closed my eyes, and the faces of friends and neighbors who I knew were praying for me drifted across my mind. My heart swelled with love and gratitude for our church family, and for the Divine Providence that had led to my discovery of the Science of Mind.

* * *

After quitting my job as a security consultant, I was drawn by the lure of big bucks and joined a life insurance agency just off Wilshire Boulevard's "Miracle Mile". Though I quickly sold several policies, when I went to deliver them the deals fell apart. Within three months I was three thousand dollars in debt from unearned advances against commissions.

It was a debt that grew larger in my mind with each passing day, along with a growing dislike for the work and — with myself. I was disgusted, depressed, anxious and, essentially, unemployed.

It was in the midst of this misery that I chanced upon something that was destined to change my life forever; one of those apparently insignificant little things that occur in every life.

From a newsstand at the corner of 6th and Berendo I picked up a copy of The Science of Mind Magazine. "Change your thinking, change your life," was the slogan on the masthead, and I was painfully aware of the need to change my thinking.

At a nearby sidewalk café I found an open seat and ordered a beef burrito and a bottle of Corona. Sheltered under an umbrella, I munched on the burrito, sipped the cool beer and read the magazine from cover to cover. If someone had been observing me closely they might have seen a light go on over my head, for one surely blazed within my mind.

What I read struck a chord deep within me that resonated with a "truth" about life and God that had been building quietly in me over the years. Here was a God not made in the image of man, but one viewed as Universal Mind/Spirit operating as Universal Law; a just deity that acted according to natural laws like the law of gravity, or electricity, or physics, without fear or favor.

I was reminded of a line from an Emerson essay: "There is one mind common to all men (mankind), and each is an outlet to it, and to all of it." Like iron filings drawn to a magnet, all the disparate *pieces of my spiritual journey up to that point began to come together.*

My God, I thought, here was a spiritual discipline open enough to reflect the clarity of Emerson, embrace the Socratic discipline of Ayn Rand, combine that with a fresh view of God and of Christ, and wrap it all within a scientific approach to effective prayer. They called it Religious Science.

In my hand I held the thoughts of a group of people who were engaged in a spiritual practice that was open and inviting, and did not require blind acceptance of church doctrine. Change your thinking, change your life, was a clarion call to my suffering ego and searching mind.

Curious to know where I could learn more about it, in the back I found a listing of Religious Science churches. There was one in North Hollywood not far from our apartment, and we went the following Sunday. Rev. Roger Miller stood 6'3", with a voice that could be heard clearly even when he whispered.

I don't remember what he said that day, but the words rang true and clear, unambiguous and direct, and brought a smile to my lips, and the promise of a fresh start to my bruised ego.

At the conclusion of the service he announced an eight-week "Prosperity Workshop," based on Wells of Abundance, *by E. V. Ingraham, to begin the following week. I signed up that morning and also enrolled in a beginner's class in the Science of Mind. It marked the beginning of a journey in mind and spirit that was destined to change my life — forever.*

6

The muted sounds of the ICU whispered their assurance that all was well. I felt little pain, and that only when I tried to move, which was seldom. Thankful to be alive, I was content to let the quiet of the moment fill my senses. Lulled by the steady beep of my heart monitor I slept.

I awoke sometime during the night, startled by what felt like two hands cradling my buttocks. They moved as though they were gently adjusting my hips and pelvis. I looked to see who it might be, but there was no one in the room.

The hands continued their movements for several long moments, while my heart nearly burst with the wonder of it. Then, as though they had accomplished what they came to do, they were gone, and I was left wondering ... who, or what, had laid those comforting hands on me.

I was *alone* in the room, yet obviously not alone. There was an unseen *Presence* with wise and loving hands that brought their healing touch to my broken body.

Astonishing as was the coincident occurrence of the earthquake and the message of Psalm 18, what had just happened was unimaginable. But it was not a figment of my imagination, I was awake! I *felt* those hands, the manipulation of my hips, the healing touch.

Wonder of wonders, what had I done to deserve such a blessing? I had no answer, but strongly felt that both events were signs of an Intelligent Presence actively engaged in my healing, assuring me that all was well.

Throughout the next day my thoughts kept returning to those healing hands, evidence of the nearness of the divine Presence. I savored them and, caught up in the spell they cast, was uplifted.

But that night, my fourth in intensive care, I had a dream — a vision — so real, so profound, that it changed me at the deepest level of my being. It wrought an alchemy of soul and mind that revealed a view of life so complete, so convincing, I felt it had to arise from that point of light where creature and Creator are one — a burst of Cosmic Consciousness.

The vision:

In the near distance was a massive stone building surrounded by an expanse of manicured lawn, dotted with ancient oak trees — a place of monastic tranquility.

A dozen monks strolled about the grounds in pairs, conversing quietly. I moved as an unseen observer from one pair to another and listened to their talk, the pattern of which was always the same.

One would make a statement; take a position on an issue as a matter of absolute truth. The other would always initially agree with the premise, saying, "Yes, that's true, but do you see?" And then, step by gentle step, with irrefutable logic, would carry the initial assertion to the exact opposite position as being equally true.

The breathtaking truth of it struck me like a bolt of lightning, and a flash of insight coursed through my body like an electric shock. I was awestruck. My mind on fire with the exquisite Truth of it, I exclaimed "Wow! That's it! That's it!"

The blazing clarity of it left me breathless. In that instant the world of duality, of opposites, in which we commonly live and move and have our being was completely replaced by one of unity — a Sublime Wholeness.

The power of it swept over me like a tsunami. Every cell of my body was alive with it — exultant! There was only the One, the All-ness of God, and Life and everything! Nothing and no one was left out. Everything fit into a seamless Whole.

In an instant I was wide awake, filled with the awesome truth of what I had just experienced. Wrapped in the wonder of it, I tried to recapture the essence of the monk's dialogue.

37

I could not. Their words fled like morning mist before the rising sun, but my *soul* and my *body* — *knew* — had *felt* — Wholeness. That *feeling* was now deeply embedded in the memory of my entire being. It would never leave me.

This indescribable experience, plus the mysterious healing hands of the previous night and the message of Psalm 18, filled me with a sense of wonder and gratitude that was simply overwhelming. Familiar words from the 16th Psalm sang in my head:

"I bless the Lord who gives me counsel; in the night also my heart instructs me. Because he is at my right hand, I shall not be moved.
Therefore my heart is glad, and my soul rejoices; my body also dwells secure."

Again, I slept.

I awoke replaying — re-living — the drama of the vision. The revelation breathed life into a symbol that, for me, is the most complete conception of God — the Yin/Yang of Taoism. It consists of two fish-like figures, identical in size and shape, one white the other black, with each containing a spot of the opposite. The figures flow naturally one into the other, depicting the interplay of paired energies — feminine/ masculine ever-present in nature, and in the world at large. All of it is held within a circle, the oldest symbol for God, suggesting how

Wholeness plays out — is seen as — pairs of opposites in the world — and in our lives.

The monks' dialogue, and the Taoist symbol, coupled with the profound sense of God's Oneness — Wholeness — revealed in the *vision* changed my view of opposites forever. Where I had previously believed they were separate, contentious, either/or, right or wrong, good or bad; it was now clear that they are inseparable, like two ends of the same stick. One cannot exist without the other; hot/cold, inside/outside, love/hate, ad infinitum. My view of life, of people, of the world, was marked with an increased clarity — a greater openness — to what lay just behind the appearance of things. It was a major shift in sight — insight — into the world around me and within.

I felt closer to the Truth, to a sense of God's presence than I ever had. Having had not one but three numinous events within the space of four nights my soul lay as open and vulnerable as my broken body. But, glory be, imprinted in my body and soul was the *experience* — the *feeling* of — Wholeness.

7

Early evening of the fifth day they moved me out of intensive care. Barbara was waiting in the hall holding Bryan. I began to laugh and cry at the same time. Barbara held Bryan close enough for me to hug and kiss him as I fought back the tears. His tiny fist was wrapped around the stem of a single yellow flower. "This is for you, daddy," he said.

Somehow my voice got past the lump in my throat.

"Thank you, buddy. I miss you," I whispered.

"I miss you too, daddy. You coming home now?"

"Not yet, buddy, but soon."

A nurse stood nearby, her attention shifting nervously from our happy, tear-streaked reunion to the empty hall.

"They sneaked us in. I'll be back later," Barbara whispered.

I didn't want to let go of my son, having come so close to never seeing him again. My lips brushed his soft cheek. "I love you, buddy."

"I love you too, daddy," he said as she lifted him from my arms. In the next moment they were gone. I held the blossom up to my nose, breathing in its faint fragrance, as my thoughts drifted back to a time just before he entered our lives.

***

Barbara and I had just moved to a new condo in Thousand Oaks when one Friday evening after dinner and a few drinks we awaited a call from a friend who had bought a new sailboat. He expected to take delivery the next day and had invited us to help sail the boat up the coast from Marina del Rey to Channel Islands Marina. We were enthusiastically contemplating what fun it would be, when the phone rang.

It was our friend, who sadly reported that the delivery of his boat was delayed, and plans for tomorrow had to be postponed. It was disappointing but we were in high spirits and, after a brief pause, I drank the last of a pony of Drambuie and said, "Why don't we drive to Las Vegas and get married?"

My question left her speechless for a moment, a condition not common with Barbara. But then wide-eyed, with a great grin on her face, she said, "Now? Are you serious?"

"Sure. Why not?"

With lightning speed she packed an overnight bag, tossed it in the trunk of our five-year-old Impala convertible, and we headed east.

We drove through the night. There was a point during the eight-hour drive when the late hour, and the diminishing glow of the evening's libations began to wear off, and with it the spontaneity that had given birth to the idea.

I muttered something like, "What the hell are we doing? Do you really want to get married? Things have been going along okay."

She had been half asleep, but she heard my words. Her face clouded up, and her eyes filled with tears, "You don't want to get married, do you? I knew it!" And now she was crying full out.

I felt awful. I could never stand to see a woman cry, especially someone I cared for.

"Hey, I'm sorry, Barb! Of course we're going to get married."

Not sure what to believe, she sat silent.

"At last, we're almost there." I breathed a tired sigh as the outlines of the city appeared on the horizon. It was nearly dawn when we drove down the world-famous strip, past the Desert Inn, where Howard Hughes was holed up on the entire top floor.

We passed a variety of gaily decorated wedding chapels to the center of town and parked near the Golden Nugget. Exhausted and hungry we had some breakfast and then, since the city offices did not open their doors until 8:00 o'clock, tried our luck at nickel slots. I won a five-dollar jackpot and took that as a good sign. If I didn't put it all back in the slot machines, it would pay the fee for our marriage license.

I didn't, and at eight-thirty sharp, with license in hand, we stood before the local magistrate and exchanged vows. He pronounced us husband and wife, I kissed my bride and we returned to the slots. It was July 13, 1967, Independence Day had come and gone.

As things turned out, there was a fated quality to my off-the-cuff suggestion that we go to Vegas and get married, for the following September Barbara was pregnant. And in the early hours of May 30, 1968, I sat in the lobby of Valley Hospital in Thousand Oaks waiting to be called to her side.

I was busy jotting down some words to capture my feelings, when a nurse beckoned. She led me down the quiet, softly-lit corridors to the nursery. She pointed a tiny bundle of white in the bed next to the window and said "Take a look at your handsome son."

And there he was — himself — looking for all the world like a miniature of my father. I looked into his eyes and felt that we had known each other forever, and a deep and hungry chasm in my heart was suddenly filled. There was a bond of love born in that instant the like of which I had never before felt.

I followed the nurse to where Barbara waited with open arms and a huge grin on her face.

"Did you see him?" She asked, her face beaming.

"I did! He looks just like Pop!"

"That means he looks like you, you fool."

"He does that! He has all his fingers and toes and is strong and handsome, just like his father."

I took her in my arms and held her close.

"Are you okay?" I asked.

"I'm fine, but tired. I'm ready to rest."

We kissed. *"I'll let you do just that. I'll take another look at our son and then I'm going to get some sleep too. I'll see you tomorrow."*

"Okay!" She said, her eyelids already closing.

On the way out I paused again at the nursery. Bryan was awake, his eyes as blue as my father's. "Hey, guy," I whispered. "Welcome!"

I walked out of the hospital, a new spring in my step, and looked up at the night sky. The night — cleaner —- sweeter; a thin sliver of silver hung on a blanket of indigo — new moon — new life. And God saw all He had made — and It was good — It was very good.

8

They rolled my bed into a semi-private room, where a bed of a different kind awaited, one with interlaced canvas strips instead of a mattress. Several young people were assembled, three on each side, for the task of moving me from one bed to the other. My heart nearly stopped when one of them, in their mighty struggle, lost her grip on my shoulder and I felt myself drop toward the floor. Terrified, I frantically gripped the guy on my right side. I felt his knees buckle but he managed to hold on and, together with the others, ultimately got my 240 pounds settled on those canvas strips.

By then my heart was pumping wildly, the image of my broken body lying in a tangled heap on the floor vivid in my mind. Christ, I thought, that was close! A nurse checked my blood pressure and pulse rate, and gave me a shot to cool me down.

My new bed had a metal framework over it, from which a chain was connected to a sling around my hips with a turnbuckle that hung just over my abdomen. Soon after the young people left a doctor came by to give it enough turns to snug the sling around my hips, and I was left alone.

When my racing heart settled, I couldn't help but laugh at the memory of a warning my dad often aimed my way for something that I did, or failed to do, as I was growing up. *"You keep that up,"* he would say, *"and you're going to get your ass in a sling."*

I lay there thinking how strange it was to have dad's colorful slang warning actually come true — my ass in a sling. Wrapped around my hips it actually felt good, like a pair of comforting arms. But where were the doctors? Why hadn't they come to talk to me?

As though summoned by my thoughts, the same doctor who visited me briefly in intensive care to test my reflexes came striding though the door. He was Dr. Michael Donato, Chief of Surgery, and he radiated a quiet self-confidence and power one hopes to find when in need of such skill. He paused at the foot of my bed to check my chart and then moved to the side of my bed where he checked the tension in the sling.

He looked at me and said, "You have probably figured out that this device is intended to gradually cinch your pelvis back into a more normal position."

"Yes, I did, and I'm wondering how long it will take, and will I be able to walk again?"

"We don't know how long; we intend to go slow and watch the progress. And, yes, I believe you will walk again. We were encouraged with the results of my brief check of you the other night; the fact that you could move your toes told us there was no permanent nerve damage.

When we get your pelvis bones back into some reasonable shape, we expect it will take surgery to pin them into position. It's all going to take time, Mr. Tuttle, so you need to be patient." He cracked a smile, "No pun intended."

"Thank you, doctor, and I'm Ed, Mr. Tuttle is my father."

The smile broadened, "Okay, Ed it is. You're doing remarkably well, keep it up."

"You can count on it, doctor," I said, and he left.

This was still fresh in my mind when Barbara walked in. When I told her they had nearly dropped me in the move from one bed to the other she was furious.

"My God, you could have been right back in intensive care.'

"Yeah, I could, or worse. I can tell you it scared the hell out of me, but it's over now and no harm done," I said; then to make light of it added, "Lucky I didn't have a heart attack."

47

"That's not funny, Ed."

She wasn't smiling. Tears welled up in her eyes, and I felt like a stupid clod when I realized how little thought I'd given to her fear and suffering with all that had happened.

"I'm sorry, hon. That was dumb. But hey," I said, spreading my arms expansively, "I'm out of intensive care, and the doctor was just here. Things are looking up."

She shook her head, took a tissue from her purse and wiped the tears from her eyes.

"Yes, that's wonderful," she said, and there was a long pause.

"But?" I waited for the other shoe to drop.

"But, I haven't told you what the doctors said about your injuries and your recovery.

"Lay it on me. What did they say?"

"To begin with, they said you might never walk again."

"Well, the doctor was just here and he seems to think that I will."

"But they said you could be in the hospital for as long as eighteen months."

"Well, he did say it would take some time, but eighteen months? No way, they've got to be kidding."

"They were *not* joking, they said you're going to need two or three more operations, something about pinning your pelvis together and resetting your left leg. They said they were too involved in trying to save your life to give that their full attention and, you may even need a third operation. I forget what that was about, it's all simply too much."

I took a deep breath. "Is that it? Is that all of it?"

"Well," she said, with some hesitation, "They also said you might never have sex again."

"Ah! Now they've gone too far." I groaned attempting a lecherous grin.

"God, can't you be serious for once?"

"Yes, my love, I can be serious, but I'm not ready to accept the doctor's limited view of my healing — or my future. That's in God's hands."

"I know," she cried, "but damn it, where was God before you hit that tree?"

Then suddenly, like a dam collapsing, all the pent-up fear, worry and anger of the past week burst forth in a flood of tears, and an anguished wail, "Why? Why did this have to happen, now, to you, to us? Ask your God that!"

"Oh Babe, come here," I said, opening my arms.

She leaned over and I wrapped my arms around her while tears stung my own eyes and a lump of sadness filled my throat.

"I can't imagine," I whispered, "what an awful time this has been for you, but we're going to get through it. I know we will."

More from utter exhaustion than from my assurances she finally stopped crying, and stood silent, watchful, waiting. The trauma of fear and sadness of the past week had etched new lines around her eyes and mouth.

"But you know Barb, it does no good to ask 'Why me, God?' Neither God nor anyone else made me get on that bike."

She picked up her purse and with a weary sigh, said, "I know. I've got to go. I'll see you tomorrow."

"Give Bryan a kiss for me and you get some rest."

She gave me a tired wave, and as she reached the door, I said, "Hey, Babe, do you know what I think God's answer to the question 'Why me, God?' would be?"

She paused waiting for the punch line she knew was coming.

He would say, "Why not you?"

She shook her head and quietly closed the door behind her.

My snappy quip aside, her words hung in the air. Why, indeed did this have to happen, to us now? Why, when we finally had begun to taste the fruits of success, had this happened? Beginning with my discovery of the Science of Mind, and the lessons I learned in the Prosperity Workshop, our lives had changed immediately for the better. Now what?

The events of that early day in May, 1966, that marked the beginning of the change, played across my mind.

***

After my abortive career in life insurance sales, I decided to explore opportunities more suited to my prior experience. I talked with security managers of some major companies in the San Fernando Valley and was referred to Tom Wathe, owner and president of a small firm supplying security guards and patrol services. A phone call got me an appointment.

His company was headquartered in a 1930s bungalow in Van Nuys, a short drive from our apartment in North Hollywood. I parked between a small white Dodge with the letters "Patrol Service" on the door, and a three-year-old Cadillac, and entered. He stood behind his desk as I was ushered in. We shook hands and he motioned me to a seat.

His well-tailored three-piece suit, white shirt and tie, plus his easy but formal manner spoke to me of his being a mid-western transplant. I took him to be a few years younger than me. Not your typical laid-back Californian, he got right to the business at hand.

The company had grown to a point where he needed someone to relieve him of customer service and sales activities, someone who could generate new growth. Thirty minutes into the interview, he concluded that I was that someone, and offered me the job.

It paid five hundred dollars a month salary plus commissions on new sales. It was lower than I had anticipated but the chemistry between us was good and the combination of customer service and sales felt like a good match with my previous experience. I began work the following day, May 5, 1966.

Fired up by what I was learning in the Science of Mind and the prosperity class, I plunged into the new job with an enthusiasm I had not felt in a long time, and a determination to prove for myself how effective were the principles we were studying. With that in mind, when a luxurious two-bedroom apartment opened up at our complex with a monthly rent of $207.00, nearly half my monthly base salary, I signed up for it. In a leap of faith I said to myself, This stuff either works or it doesn't, but I'm going to find out — and I did.

My enthusiasm, a word derived from en theos — in God — knew no bounds. My working title was Manager of Field Services and, from the start, our relationship was more like that of partners than employer/employee. Our objective was to supply the very best service available at competitive prices, with close and frequent contact with all our current customers as the hallmark.

With minimal direction from Tom, I was given free rein and, early on, revised our sales proposal by moving the price of our service from opening paragraphs to the last page, and offering a "free" security survey to identify any weaknesses in the prospect's current security posture.

At the end of the first month Tom raised my salary one hundred dollars, and at the end of the second month he raised it another hundred and, at the end of the third month he increased it by three hundred more. In three short months my base salary had doubled, not counting commissions on new sales.

I had all the proof I needed, this Science of Mind stuff really worked!

Early one evening, while we were having a drink after work, Tom said he wasn't sure he wanted the company to grow much beyond its current level of sales, $1,500,000.00 annually. His comment reminded me of when, as a private detective, I had earned $15,000.00 my first year, double what I had been paid, as a Detective Sergeant, and had foolishly thought I would be happy with that level of income for the balance of my working life.

I didn't respond to Tom's musing but a different idea was taking shape in my mind. I had recently learned how easily and irrationally we place limitations on what we can achieve, and then act as though they are holy writ, inscribed in stone. I knew better now and was ready to implement my plan — my vision of growth.

9

Still Barbara's question hung in the air, and in my mind; *why?* I was a skilled rider, and was not hot-dogging. My study and practice of Science of Mind had convinced me that everything, all of creation, is subject to Universal Law. Nothing happens by chance, there are no accidents, only the interplay of cause and effect at the heart of every event. It's a hard truth to live by for it strips us of all our favorite excuses, especially of blaming God for every sad or miserable thing that comes along. But the astounding psychic events that I experienced while in intensive care presented a new aspect that went beyond my sense of the working of God's Law. They brought an element into the situation that could only be described as a manifestation of God's Grace — God's Love.

And though I had demonstrated a certain proficiency in my understanding and application of God's Law, God's Love and Grace remained a mystery. *What had I done to merit God's Love and Grace,* I wondered? But then a moment later, like a news flash it struck me; God does not measure our worthiness, like some shopkeeper assesses the size of his bank account, but accepts and loves us as his sons and daughters just as we are — warts and all.

And I could not but feel the presence of God's invisible hand in the total experience. Although I did not know the *why* of it, I strongly felt that it was an essential element in my soul's journey, a tempering and maturing of my understanding — my faith. If so, what did God have in mind? What was I to learn from it?

The first answer was abundantly clear and it filled me with a sense of joy that was boundless; *it was good to be alive!*

This simple, powerful truth struck me my first day out of intensive care, when a young man placed a basin of hot water on the tray table next to my bed, along with a washcloth and a face towel. He dipped the washcloth into the hot water, wrung out most of it and handed it to me.

"I thought you might like to wipe your face." He spoke softly, his manner light and caring. "My name is John," he said.

I took the washcloth from his hand and pressed it against my face from my hairline to my chin. The feel of it against my skin was so exquisite, so comforting I could hardly bear it; so overcome that words failed me. John seemed to understand, for each time I reluctantly handed the washcloth back to him, he dipped it in the water and returned it to me.

I could not get enough of it. It was as though every cell of my body shouted in exaltation, *My God, it's good to be alive!*

When the water cooled he handed me the face towel, and I wiped my face dry. He gathered up the basin, washcloth, and towel and, pointing to the badge on his shirt, said again, "I'm John. You need anything, you ask for me." And he left.

Never was I so intensely aware of what a gift life is, just how vibrant and precious — and fragile. I would never open my eyes to another sunrise — another dawn — without the memory of that moment, that realization rising within me, like the rising sun itself, to light yet another day.

It reminded me of an episode that involved a dog named Laddie, a beautiful, tri-color border-collie. It was 1949. Eleanore and I had been married only a short time when her sister and brother-in-law gave the dog. He was not yet full grown.

***

He had not yet reached his first birthday when I carried him into the clinic and laid him gently on the examining table. The examination was brief and thorough. "He's very ill," the doctor said. "He has hepatitis, a virulent form. I'm afraid we may be too late.

My heart sank within me; he was so young — just a puppy — and vulnerable. I fought back the tears and asked, "What can we do?"

"Well, there's nothing I can do here that you can't do at home," he said, and handed me a bottle of pills. "These may help. Give him one in the morning and another at night until they are all gone. I hope it works.

Laddie lay motionless on the table, his soft brown eyes fixed on me with a look of utter trust. Mine were filled with tears. I picked him up, carried him to the car and laid him beside me on the front seat. He had not uttered a single whimper during the whole time.

When we arrived home, Eleanore was waiting at the door; she held it open as I entered with Laddie in my arms.

"It's not good," I said, answering the question in her eyes. "He has hepatitis, and the doctor doubts that he will recover. He gave me some medicine for him, and said he hoped it would work." I placed his limp body gently on the bed of blankets we had made for him in a corner of the small kitchen. "The doctor said that he was to be fed cooked ground beef and rice, and nothing else ever."

"That's no problem," she said, "if it will help him get well."

Each morning and evening of the days that followed I opened Laddie's mouth and placed the pill as far back on his tongue as I could, and then held his muzzle shut until I was sure he had swallowed it. As sick as he was, the ground beef and rice got his attention and he ate a little from time to time, but the days passed with no visible change in his condition.

57

Every day I carried him outside and placed him on the grass to do his business. One afternoon, after many long days of watching, and caring, and waiting, for what seemed to be the inevitable, I carried him out and placed him on the grass, where he stood on trembling legs.

Indian summer was upon us, blessing the world with an exquisite mixture of warm sun and brisk, autumn wind. A stiff breeze buffeted and carried a colorful array of radiant fallen leaves over the New Jersey landscape.

Laddie somehow managed to maintain his balance on unsteady legs, his nose pointed into the wind. As I watched, he lifted his head and sniffed the air, his legs steadied under him, and I saw something I hadn't seen for many days — he wagged his tail! I'll never know what it was that he smelled on the wind, but In that moment I knew — knew without a doubt — Laddie was going to live. It was as though he decided to live.

I could hardly believe my eyes. I yelled, "Yes! Thank you, God!" My cry of joy brought my wife running from the house. "What's wrong, what's happened?" she cried.

"Look at him!" I shouted. "He decided to live!"

She clapped her hands and laughed, even as tears poured from her eyes. She shook her head in amazement, "He's decided to live?"

"Yes!" I roared; "He decided to live!"

And live he did, eating ground beef and rice all the days of his long life.

10

Caught up in the memory I whispered "Me too, Laddie. Me too!" But even as I said the words I was struck with the realization that it took a host of people and a series of interrelated events even to present me with anything approaching choice in the matter. Once again I was face-to-face with the same question I had first asked myself on that far-away island in the South Pacific with comrades falling all around me.

Why? Who, or what, really chooses who is to live and who is to die? An entirely different question than the one Barbara asked, but not unrelated. Only God has the answer to this one and, surrendering to the ultimate mystery we are likely to respond — *it's God's will!*

I've heard it said that God will sometimes put a man flat on his back, so he can look into his face. Well, I was certainly flat on my back, but I could only guess at what it was that God was looking for in my face. I suspect that it is always change of some kind that He looks for; why else would he put a man flat on his back?

Change! The word reverberated like a clap of thunder in my head. Change? I couldn't believe my ears, or my mind, or wherever the word came from. If change was what was needed, did it have to come in such a drastic way? Couldn't a gentle nudge have done the trick? Was I so blind, so hard to reach, so satisfied with myself that it took *this* to get my attention?

The answer to that was so obvious I couldn't deny it. Truth is, I *was* blind, hard to reach, self-satisfied and, God help me, proud of it.

But a short week ago I was an ambitious, hard-driving executive, nearing the top of my game, a full-blown, in-your-face alpha-male. I was a self-sufficient guy who knew where he was going and how to get there. No one, and nothing, was going to stand in my way. Then in a single instant *everything* changed, and with it my very existence.

Where I had been strong, independent, self-assured, impervious to the slings and arrows that others suffered in their journey through life, I now lay helpless, completely dependent on others for my every need — for my very survival.

And from that eye-opener there came another single-word answer — *Humility!* Ah, now there was a virtue that was sadly lacking in my life! From my earliest years there was little

60

in my character or sense of self that could be called humble. Quite the contrary.

From as early as I could remember I had been filled with an unspoken but persistent sense that I was *different* — *special* — and that people generally sensed this about me. Though this sounds like the blather of a monumental ego it was not something that I openly spoke of or acted out, it was more a *feeling* — an inner sense — that I quietly, secretly, accepted as though confirmed by the heavens — by right of birth.

Considering the time, place, and state of affairs of my arrival on this plane of existence there was little about it that was remarkable, except for the fact than it happened on a day when millions paused in their activities to offer up prayers of thanks to God for the blessings they received.

***

I was born In the early morning hours of Thanksgiving Day, November 29, 1923, to Edward Winand Tuttle and Lila Mae Ackerman-Tuttle. I was told the doctor and I arrived at the same instant, though he had the more difficult time of it traveling by horse and carriage over the New Jersey hills from Boonton, through the winter night to attend his patient. He arrived safely, as did I.

In their joy they named me Edward Van Valkenburg (can you believe it?) Tuttle. It was my fate to be named after a hero in a book one of my aunts was reading, a decision that I am sure led directly to my being dubbed "Sonny." I found that to be lot better than growing up as "little Eddie" or "Junior," nicknames I would have hated. So, Sonny it was, and when everyone around me shortened it to "Son," I could live with that.

We lived in a little three-room clapboard house, built on a piece of land carved from my grandfather's farm, in Taylortown, New Jersey. It wasn't really a town, it was a cross-roads village built loosely around the intersection of Rockaway Valley Road and Route 202, in the northern hill country of the state, a collection of two dozen dwellings spread loosely over a square mile.

For a blessed year-and-a-half there were just the three of us in that little house, until May 2, 1925, when my brother Clement "Harold," (Van Valkenburg wasn't so bad after all), was born, and I was no longer the only begotten.

***

It may well be that any child who happens to be the first-born, particularly a male-child, *feels* special. Whatever the source, whether true or fanciful, the *feeling* — the inner certainty — led again and again throughout my life to events that reinforced the belief. The earliest and, perhaps most significant event happened the year before I began school.

62

***

I was nearly seven years old when I started school; my mother had chosen not to send me until my brother Clem, who was not yet five, could go too. I don't know why she did that, probably thought that we could watch out for each other, but it turned out especially well for me.

Every day she taught me, and by the time Clem was ready to start school I had mastered the alphabet, could read a little and had memorized most of the multiplication tables. I could also do simple addition and subtraction.

She sometimes paused in her chores to sit by my side, her arm around my shoulders, and talk me through the task at hand. Each time I mastered a step in the process, no matter how small, I was rewarded with a smile, a touch, an encouraging word. "Son, you can learn anything you set your mind to," she would say.

I lived for that approval, and was driven to do even better.

***

There is nothing that motivates like love and encouragement. She taught me to love learning, a gift that has lasted a lifetime. But it took years of living for me to fully appreciate the enormous influence that year had in the shaping of my life — my sense of self. Everything that I have ever accomplished — *everything* — has borne the imprint of that unforgettable year. It fed my secret sense of being *special,* a feeling that was reinforced my first day in school.

63

***

It was September 1930, Clem was five years old and it had finally arrived — our first day of school. Mom went with us, Clem on one side and me on the other, as we walked the half-mile to school.

It was a new brick building, the finest in the village. It held two large rooms, but only one was ever used for classes. All eight grades met in that one room and there were twenty-two students that first day.

I sat in the front row and soon became the focus of attention when my mother told the teacher, Miss Swann, that she had taught me at home, and that I had done well.

Miss Swan was tall and slender with dark eyes, soft brown hair and a sweet manner that put me completely at ease. She was beautiful, almost as pretty as my mother. She wrote some words on the blackboard and I read them, then some numbers for me to add and subtract, and I did that, and recited some of the multiplication tables.

When I finished, Miss Swan said that I would start in the second grade. So even though we began school the same day, I still wound up a year ahead of Clem. I liked that.

11

There was not the slightest hint of humility in any of that, but humility was not a quality that was much expressed, nor highly valued, in the time and place in which I grew up. These were the years of the Great Depression; hard times had come upon the land, and FDR, Franklin Delano Roosevelt, was president.

His "New Deal" offered unemployment relief projects for the millions out of work. My Dad worked briefly on one of the C. C. C. (Civilian Conservation Corps) projects, removing diseased elm trees from nearby forests, but he was too independent of mind and spirit to be satisfied with that for long.

No stranger to either hard times or hard work, while still a child himself my father had to leave school to go to work in the local foundry to help his mother feed and clothe his brothers and sisters. He was only ten years old; ten years old and he worked ten hours a day in a foundry. No one had to tell him about hard times.

During all those lean years we made only one trip to the local welfare agent. It was widely reported that there was a surplus of some basic foodstuffs available for pickup at the home of the county agent.

***

Dad knew the guy by name, and also where he lived. The items were stored at the man's property, and my dad took me with him to check it out.

We pulled into the driveway, past the house, and up to the barn in the back. There were no other cars or people around, but it was only a couple minutes later when we heard a door slam in the house and a man emerged and walked our way. He was tall, over six feet, past middle age and very heavy. He could be heard huffing and puffing his way up the driveway, the buttons of his white shirt hanging on for dear life to cover his belly, and the fly of his pants engaged in the same mighty struggle. He had obviously not missed many meals.

It turned out that he was as mean-tempered as he was fat. In a gravelly wheeze that seemed to come from somewhere deep within the folds of fat, he growled, "I suppose you're here for the handouts."

I could see the flush of color building above my dad's collar, but his reply was quiet enough as he said, "Well, Henry, I heard that the government had some surplus foodstuffs available for pickup here."

"Might be," Fat Henry said, "and who are you?"

Offering his hand, "I'm Ed Tuttle. Live up in Taylortown."

The man reached out and grasped my dad's hand. I watched the muscles in my dad's forearm bulge, and the look of surprise and pain on Henry's face as he grunted, "What do you need?"

66

"What have you got?"

Without another word, Henry opened the barn doors an, brought out a sack of flour, a tub of margarine, and a large block of cheese wrapped in wax paper. Gasping for breath like a fish out of water he handed each one to my dad, who put them on the back seat of our car. It seemed to pain Henry to part with the "hand-outs," like they were coming out of his own store. Embarrassed for my dad, I was choked with anger. He was a better man than Fat Henry would ever be.

It was an unforgettable experience. The "free" foodstuffs came at too high a price — our dignity and self-respect. My dad must surely have felt it too, especially with my being there. Neither of us said a word about it, but we never went for another "free" handout there — or anywhere else.

* * *

I learned that poverty is not a matter of how much money you earn, or the cash you have in your pocket, but it is the measure of love and support you receive from those around you. In all the important ways, we were rich! And hard times, like everything else in life, brought their own blessing; they were apt to make you tough, resilient, a survivor; grateful for the good that came your way — but not humble.

12

The one activity where I might have learned something about humility, attending church, did not play large in my young years, with but one exception. I was about eleven and Clem a year-and-half younger when mom made her surprise announcement.

* * *

"You and your brother Clem are going to be attending Catholic Catechism class, and make your First Communion."

I looked closely at my mom to see if she was serious. She was.

"Why?" I asked, puzzled.

"Because when your father and I were married in the Rectory at Our Lady of Mt. Carmel Church by Monsignor Delaney, I had to promise that you boys would be raised Catholic. Me being a Protestant, and not wanting to convert like my sister Kate, I had to make that promise. And a promise is a promise."

"Where are we going to do that?"

"They hold the classes in the Parochial School right across the street from your grandmother Mary."

"When?"

"You start next week." And so we did.

We were team-taught by two nuns. They were both tall for women, or it may be their black garments made them appear that way. We learned quickly enough that you didn't want to tangle with the older one; she always carried a long ruler and did not hesitate to apply it.

"Martin, pay attention!" … Whack!

"James, stand up when you're called upon." … Whack!

I thought the younger Sister was very pretty, her face picture-framed by the white cowl and black head cover.

It wasn't difficult to satisfy them; we simply memorized the prayers and creeds they taught. Succeed at that and we had the answer to any question they might ask, word-for-word — just the way they wanted to hear it.

Joining our classmates in attendance at the nine o'clock Mass on Sunday was one of the requirements. One Sunday as I watched those who were receiving Communion take the wafer on their tongue, it struck me that it must taste like a piece of cardboard. An empty stomach did the rest; the image made me sick and I fainted dead away. The younger Sister came to my rescue. She took me next door to the Rectory, where she gave me some tea and a sweet roll — and I was healed.

I never cared much for the Catholic Church. It always had a strange feel to it. The service was not in English, and the image of Jesus they prayed to was a lot different than the one I had seen in Presbyterian Sunday School.

69

Instead of a strong, blue-eyed, blond, healthy guy with a smile on his face, surrounded by children, they had a dark-haired emaciated man hanging on a cross, with a crown of thorns jammed on his head. They called him the "Man of Sorrows," and the name fit the image.

The whole scene was dark and grim, like it was meant to scare the hell out of us, and hell was where we were headed, they said, if we didn't pay attention. They said that we were all sinners, right from birth — Original Sin they called it. I couldn't help but wonder how a new-born babe could be a sinner. They put the fear in God-fearing.

I figured I might get around to understanding it, but for the time being all I had to do was to learn the words and act like I understood them — believed them. I can tell you there was a part of me that wanted to believe, even tried to believe, but that didn't happen.

In the end Clem and I fulfilled Mom's promise to the priest. Having done that, it was rare thereafter to find us in Our Lady of Mt. Carmel Catholic Church, except for baptisms and funerals, and thankfully there were few of those.

During those same years we were introduced to another vision of Jesus when, on rare occasions, Grandma Laura would take Clem and me to the small white chapel in our village. There we read stories of how Jesus fed the multitudes and healed the sick.

This Jesus seemed like the kind of guy you would like to meet; a tall, sun-tanned, blue-eyed man with long, honey-blond hair and a smile on his face. He went about healing people.

After hearing a lesson about Jesus we sat on hard wooden benches while the visiting preacher warned everyone that if we didn't mend our ways we were going to go straight to hell. That was something we had learned in the Catholic Church, but the minister was really worked up over the possibility; you could almost smell the fire and brimstone.

But with just us kids and a half-dozen ancient, white-haired, ladies within the range of his voice, none of whom seemed capable of committing the kind of sins that would get them a ticket to hell, I figured he must be practicing for his next stop.

Like an old wind-up phonograph he would finally come to a stop and, with one last warning, send us on our way. One of the ladies always gave us a fresh orange to take home. I never saw any man in attendance.

***

None of the people I loved and looked up to were strong on going to church, but you would have to look long and hard to find a better collection of individuals to have as family and neighbors — as examples of how to live a faith-centered life.

As a lot they tended to mind their own business, their word was their bond, and their handshake as good as a signed document. They met life as they found it, asked favor of no one, and communed with the Almighty in their own fashion, time, and place. Not given much to humility but good men, and that was good enough for me.

13

"Are you awake?"

I opened my eyes to a vision of fresh loveliness in a starched white uniform. "I am now!"

The nurse smiled. "We have to check on you once in a while, you know," she said as she strapped a blood pressure cup on my arm and placed a thermometer under my tongue.

"Have any pain?"

"No," I mumbled around the thermometer.

"Need anything to help you sleep?" she asked, as she checked my temperature.

"No, I don't think so."

Making notations on the chart that hung at the foot of my bed, she said, "Hit the button if you need anything."

"I will." My eyes never left her face.

"You're doing fine!" Her smile lit up the room. As she opened the door to leave, her slender body was backlit by lights from the hall. I've always been a sucker for a pretty woman in a nurse's uniform. Some things never change.

So, here I lay, having dodged yet another bullet but faced with a challenge every bit as daunting as surviving combat. I was older and wiser, and armed with a faith I had not then possessed, for then my concept of God was indistinct, a blurred mixture of childhood images and adult questioning, fuzzy and immature. That hadn't stopped me from praying when the occasion arose, like hugging the ground in a shallow foxhole on Peleliu while the Japanese tried to kill us with a barrage of high-explosive artillery shells. But I was more of a fatalist then, than a believer. Once I accepted the fact that I was either going to make it or I wasn't, there was no benefit in worrying or praying about it.

In retrospect, the closest I came to a God-centered pattern of living I did not find in church, but in the Boy Scouts of America.

* * *

I could hardly wait until I was twelve years old so I could join Troop 113. Hard times or no, my mother, bless her soul, made sure I had a proper uniform shirt, and I was on my way. The Scout oath and law worked their way into my mind and into my spirit;

On my honor I will do my best
To do my duty to God and my country
And to obey the Scout Law;
To help other people at all times;
To keep myself physically strong,
Mentally awake, and morally straight.

These words were challenge enough for anyone to live by, and I took the Scout motto, "Be prepared," to mean self-reliant, a major goal in my young life. And Scouting offered something else I did not find in church — fun.

There were overnight or weekend camping trips where we learned how to build a campfire and cook our own food; my specialties were spaghetti with meat sauce, or "Mulligan" stew.

One autumn night on a camp-out, with just a single, thread-bare blanket I thought I would freeze to death. Sleep was out of the question. I got up, wrapped myself in the blanket, and settled next to the campfire. I stoked the fire regularly and, by turning my body like a roast on a skewer, survived the night. I was never so glad to see the sun come up.

But the activity I most enjoyed was when a professional boxer, Joe Murphy, came to teach us the manly art of self defense. I was a natural, and learned quickly how to move like a fighter; a kind of easy shuffle with my left foot always leading. I learned how to throw a punch with my whole body behind it.

"Tuttle," Joe would whisper in his gravelly voice, "keep your hands up, and your chin tucked in behind your left shoulder."

"Okay, Mr. Murphy," I would grunt.

"Breathe boy, breathe and jab! Get that left straight out there with your body behind it. That's it.

Good! A good jab keeps your opponent off-balance and sets him up for a hard right hook. There was never a fighter worth his weight who did not have a good left jab."

I was in my glory, intent on becoming a brainy boxer — quick, smart, and tough. I got into the habit of carrying a couple sets of sixteen-ounce gloves on the lookout for anyone who was interested in sparring a couple rounds. Ring Magazine was my favorite piece of reading, and when I wasn't boxing I was reading about boxers.

The skills I learned not only filled me with a new measure of self-confidence, they were to serve me well in later years in the Marines and in the State Police. But at the time my head was filled with dreams of winning the Golden Gloves, and going professional. I never did, thank God, but that didn't stop me from dreaming.

Like most youngsters, dreaming of what I might be and do when I grew up often filled my mind, but during those years, dreaming of what the future held was not limited to us kids. The harsh reality of the Depression, the general lack of money and work, set the adults to dreaming as well.

It was not uncommon to hear grownups, with a distant look in their eyes, speak of a future when their ship would come in. It was a magic ship, of course, a metaphor for the return of better times. When possessions are few and opportunity scarce, there is little left but to dream of better times to come.

Although everyone seemed to be in the same boat, at least everyone I knew, there was an unquenchable spirit of hope for the future. We lived in the greatest country in the world; America was still the land of opportunity. We might be down, but you better not count us out. The music of the time, both the beat and the lyrics, reflected that spirit.

The pathos was captured in Brother, Can You Spare a Dime? Yet, also typical of the music was a song that my brother Clem and I sang as a duet our first year in school.

It was 1930 and as we approached the holidays, Miss Swann decided it would be good to present a musical program to the community, one in which we would all take part.

When we mentioned this to my mother, she was thrilled and felt it would be terrific for Clem and me to sing a duet. Now, Clem and I spent more time fighting than singing, but she had a song in mind and would not take no for an answer.

Keep Your Sunny Side Up was the song, a funny, upbeat response to the hard times. Motivated by Mom's enthusiastic direction we practiced as though we were going to audition at Radio City Music Hall.

When the evening came, most everyone in the town turned out. Clem and I stood with the others in the semi-darkened classroom, peeking through the gap between the sliding doors at the assembled crowd of neighbors and friends. Mom sat in the front row while Dad stood with some of the other men against the back wall.

"Edward," Miss Swann whispered, "you and Clement are on next." My stomach was host to a flock of butterflies, but there was no getting out of it. She opened the sliding doors just wide enough for us to slip through. My attention was fixed on my mother's face; she smiled and gave us an encouraging nod, as we stepped front and center. Standing side by side we belted out the lyrics.

Keep your sunny side up — up,
Hide the side that gets blue.
If you have nine sons in a row,
Baseball teams make money you know.
Keep your sunny side up — up,
Hide the side that gets blue — do.
Stand upon your legs —
Be like two fried eggs —
Keep your sunny side up!

Everybody clapped, and cheered, and I saw tears of pride and joy in my mother's eyes as we took our bows.

14

Nowhere in any of that could I find the slightest hint of humility and, search as I might, I couldn't find it anywhere else in all the years leading up to my collision with the tree. But if it was humility I had to learn, one could say I was in the midst of a *crash* course. The pun made me groan, but it also made me chuckle. There are times when the most healing thing you can bring to a situation is a sense of humor; even when the laugh is on you.

And then as though someone had turned a light on the matter, I realized my earliest sense of self, the inner conviction that I was *special,* had left no room for anything approaching humility. And there had been so many events and circumstances that served to reinforce this personal myth that I was not likely to deny or abandon it, or even to examine it closely. Had I done so, I might have caught a glimpse of its dark side; that nothing I did — no matter how stellar the performance or result — was good enough to satisfy the image.

I looked down the length of my body, immobile in the grasp of a canvas sling, my future uncertain, and I prayed: *Thank you, God,*

I can still think, read, feed myself, meditate — and pray. Though it fell far short of the independence that was so much a part of my core character, I was deeply grateful for these blessings.

Some relief came with a line by W. C. Handy, father of the blues, "*I ain't much God, but I'm all I've got.*" How marvelous, I thought, and laughed out loud. I suddenly felt emancipated, relieved of a burden I assumed was mine to carry forever; my personal myth with its inflated expectations was punctured like a child's balloon. I lay there unable to move but filled with a joyous sense of freedom — of release.

Then as though on cue, Barbara walked in clutching a brown paper bag, and wearing a bright smile.

"Hi," she said, giving me a kiss. "How are you doing?"

"Okay. You look like you're feeling better."

"I am; slept for ten hours straight. First full night's sleep I've had since the accident. It was wonderful!"

"Hey, that's good. What have you got in the bag?"

She produced a hand-held tape recorder, an earplug, and several cassette tapes by Rev. Joel Goldsmith.

"Hey, this is great. You know he's one of my favorites. Thanks, Baby."

"You're welcome," she said with a satisfied grin. "I can't stay long, there's too much to do at home."

"Speaking of home, how does the money situation look?

"Better than you might think; Tom said he would continue your salary."

"Wow! That's terrific, and there will be some disability income from insurance. I guess we are going to be okay, huh?"

"Yes we will. I've got it all organized, you don't have to worry about it. You just get well, we miss you at home."

"God, I miss being there."

"I know. I'll be back later." She leaned over and gave me a peck on the lips. "Get some rest."

"I'll do that; see you later then."

She turned at the door; I blew her a kiss, and she was gone.

Then, inserting a tape into the recorder, with the earplug in place, I hit the start button and closed my eyes. "Good morning!" He spoke with a slightly high pitch to his voice, a habit that conveyed a sense of excitement to what he had to share. "God's grace is sufficient unto all things,'" he said, and launched into one of his uplifting talks. I smiled to myself, content to listen.

With my life reduced to a simple narrow focus — to heal — an unexpected sense of peace and surrender filled me. Only God knew how this would unfold but I had no intention of being a passive observer. The spiritual discipline I had studied and applied over the past few years had convinced me of the incredible creative power one's thought and belief bring to bear on the outcome of any condition or situation. I had *experienced* results enough in my life to *know* the truth of that.

The incredible uplifting experiences in I.C.U., and the equally amazing chain of events that led to my timely arrival, and survival, had completely convinced me of God's healing presence and power in the situation. I spent countless hours listening to Goldsmith's mantra: *God's grace is sufficient unto all things.* I didn't understand it, my mind could not grasp it, but it was fixed in my mind, and confirmed with every beat of my heart, until I felt the perfect activity of God in everything and everyone. Everyone who approached my bed; doctors, nurses, orderlies, technicians, and every treatment, every piece of equipment, the entire hospital I felt — *believed* — to be a perfect expression of the Mind/Spirit of the Living God — the Holy Spirit. It *was* sufficient unto all things.

That night I had another dream or vision, this one of a man's ring. It was a cross contained within a circle which, as a separate piece, was mounted atop a tangle of branches. The ring was cast in gold. When I awoke, the meaning of the symbols in the dream stood out clear in my mind.

The circle is the oldest symbol for God, never-beginning and never-ending, and the cross held within it was the mark of the Christ Presence and Power. As a separate piece mounted atop a tangle of branches and thorns, symbols of life's struggles and pain, it signified an overcoming of those struggles — a rising above them — never a part of them.

Taken in its entirety for me the ring signified the Christ Consciousness in God overcoming the trials and tribulations of life; a visible statement of faith. I embraced it completely, even to the extent of tracing the image on my forehead with my thumb like a blessing every night before going to sleep. It was clear to me that upon my recovery I was to have such a ring made.

15

Shortly after I was moved to a regular room my mother flew in from New Jersey to be at my side. Though she was not entirely well, the devil himself could not have prevented her from coming. I can't begin to imagine what terrors went through her mind when she heard of my accident, my brush with death, but then I never really tried to understand. I was too filled up with myself to get past the habitual distance that was so much a part of our relationship. She loved me, this woman who bore me, worried about me, wanted to keep me safe; and I loved her as only a son can love his mother. But the ghost of the memory that gave birth to my childhood cry of pain; "*I don't need you! I don't need anyone!*" though long ago buried still made its ugly, ignorant presence felt.

There was no way I could have understood — or reacted differently — to what I *felt* that day so long ago. I was seven years old.

***

I had run all the way home from school eager, to tell Mom how happy Miss Swann was with my schoolwork.

I burst through the door "Hi, Mom!"

I stopped dead in my tracks when I saw my mother sitting on Sam Gould's lap. It felt like someone had kicked me in the stomach.

Startled and embarrassed she leaped up and came to where I stood, silent, unmoving, and reached out to touch me. I ducked away from her hand, dropped my books on the floor, and ran into the next room.

What the Hell was he doing here? I hated the bastard, a red-faced loud-mouth with the smell of booze on him and a yen for my mother.

It had been more than two years since we had last seen him, and the memory of that still burned in my gut.

He had arrived in a flashy, yellow roadster and took my mother, my baby brother Homer and me, on a trip to High Point Monument. It was bitter cold on the observation deck as the dark clouds raced overhead pushed by a wind that spewed stinging flakes of snow into my face.

I looked over to where they stood; my mother holding Homer in her arms, while Sam held her close. I hated him and was furious at my mother. I stood apart — sulking — angry, wanting only to get back in his fancy Oldsmobile and go home, which we finally did.

Sam pulled the car up into our driveway, and stopped. Mom sat in the middle next to him, with Homer on her lap, and I was next to the door. I pushed the door open to get out, but because the car sat on the slope of our driveway the door kept closing on me. I pushed it with my foot. Well maybe I kicked it. That was enough to make Sam mad, and that made my mother mad and, when we got in the house and she told Dad, he got mad. He grabbed me and gave me a spanking I would never forget. I didn't think I deserved it, and that made me mad at him, and not just for the spanking, but for what I felt he was allowing Sam to get away with. They had worked together somewhere, or had been in the Navy together, friends and shipmates.

And here he was — back again!
"Sonny," she said a sadness in her eyes. I stood stony-faced, my arms folded, a sob caught in my throat. I heard Sam mutter something that sounded like, "He'll be okay. Let him be."
"You better go, Sam. Just go!" She said. And he stalked out without another word.
She stood next to me, silent, waiting. I turned away, would not look at her. With a sigh that sounded like a sob caught in her throat, she turned and walked back into the kitchen. I knew she was afraid that I would tell Dad when he got home from work, but I never did.
Angry, hurt, confused, I shrunk within myself, seeking a place to hide from the rage and pain, the

feeling of betrayal that gripped me. A fierce coldness wrapped its bony grip around my heart and erected a wall from behind which I looked at my mother and shouted, "I don't need you! I don't need anyone!"

***

How foolish, how filled with empty bravado that all seemed now, when there was so little I could do for myself. But, as always, she ignored the awkwardness and the irritation that bubbled just beneath the surface, and loved me anyway — ungrateful lout that I was.

I had gathered from Barbara's remarks that Mom's efforts to be of help with Bryan, and the house, had met with as little welcome as had her concern for me.

I thanked her for coming and for everything she was trying to do, said that I was well on the way to a full recovery, and suggested that she was really needed more at home. She left after a week.

16

In the unbroken white of the hospital room, day after day drifted by wrapped in the sameness that marks those periods in every life where a set routine determines the activity and pace. The uniformity was interrupted only by an emergency, or an act of God, like the earthquake and, since I was restricted to a single body position, the effect was magnified. There is a strange comfort in such a circumstance for in the process, and to the extent possible, my every basic need was met. I was left with but one decision, how to respond to the situation, and was intensely aware of how critical the choice was to my recovery.

I knew there was only one sensible response: Trust in God and pour every thought, every ounce of energy, into a vision — a conviction — of full recovery. Ironically, I had just completed the academic requirements for Minister of Religious Science and thought, with a wry sense of humor, that if this was God's idea of a final examination he had outdone himself. With all of that, I longed for the day when I could again sleep on my side or stomach, or stand upright and walk.

Visits by friends from work and from church, who were like extended family, broke the set routine of the day. Mostly they were brief, as hospital visits tend to be, and bland. Those few, and few there were, who came in with sad expressions on their face, and the idea of commiserating with me over the misfortune of it all, set records for brevity. Well-intentioned they may be, but they do not lend strength to the healing process.

Most of my friends and associates knew me well enough, and were generally of a different mind-set, and our visits were pleasant and up-lifting. Two there were that I would remember with special love and gratitude.

One afternoon, shortly after I had been moved to a regular room, I was listening to one of Goldsmith's tapes when a familiar figure came through the door. He wore a soft gray hat perched squarely on his head, the front brim a canopy over sharp, gray, penetrating eyes. With the stocky build of a middleweight, and the stride of man on a mission, he was none other than the Rev. Dr. Robert J. Bitzer, President of the International Association of Religious Science Churches, and pastor of the Hollywood Church. He was also my teacher and mentor.

"I don't believe it. Dr. Bitzer, what a pleasant surprise."

"Well, no more of a surprise than for me to hear that you were in the hospital." He looked at me for a long moment. "I wanted to see for myself how you were doing."

"Well, under the circumstances, I'm doing fine."

"I can see that." Then, with just a glint of humor, he added, "You know we began our ministerial class with ten people. I want to make sure we graduate ten."

Smiling in return I said, "Let me guess, Dr. Bitzer; you're going to tell me to take up my bed and walk."

With emphasis on every syllable he replied, "Ab-so-lute-ly! It may take a bit of time, God's own time, but that's what I see."

"Me too, Dr. Bitzer, me too!"

"Then why don't we affirm that truth, right here, right now," he said.

"I'd like that very much." I closed my eyes and let his prayer wash over me — fill me.

"There is only One Power and Presence in all of creation; God, the Good Omnipotent, Source and Substance of all. We are one with that Presence and Power; conceived in It, sustained by It, and an expression of It. It is the very Life of your Life, the Energy and Intelligence of every cell of your body. It is the Holy Spirit, the Wholeness of Spirit, forever revealing Itself. We rest in that Truth, and know that all is well. We bless It, accept It, and let It be so. And so It is!"

For several moments we were silent, then I reached out and took his hand. "Thank you!"

He squeezed my hand, "You're welcome, Ed. I'll see you in class." He gave my hand a parting squeeze, and with that he was gone.

As Dr. Bitzer's visit had nourished my soul, the other special visitor would attend to my body's needs; he was Tom, my barber. He arrived one afternoon carrying a small satchel that contained the tools of his trade.

"Thought you might like a haircut and a shave," he said.

It took a moment for me to recover from the surprise and delight at seeing him. "I sure would, I'm getting downright grizzly."

"Yeah, you are. Well, let's get to it."

He placed the contents of his bag on the tray table, secured an apron around my throat and placed a towel under my head. As was my habit, I closed my eyes while he clipped and snipped. When he was satisfied he handed me a mirror.

"How does that look?"

"Great! Feels good too."

"Now let's get rid of that scrubby growth of hair on your face. You don't intend to grow a beard, do you?"

"No, I don't."

"I'll leave the mustache, just trim it a bit."

"Okay." Again I closed my eyes and surrendered to the moment. He began with a hot towel followed by fresh-scented creamy lather lavishly laid on with a brush. Then with a medley of swift sure strokes from a straight-razor, that seemed to fairly dance over my face, he removed the stubble, applied another hot towel and then a splash of Halston after-shave. It felt like he was caring for a brother, or father; I was so overwhelmed by his humanity I was unable to speak.

Aware of it, Tom was silent while he gathered up his implements.

The surge of emotion finally ebbed enough for me to reach out and take his hand. "Thanks, Tom. I feel brand-new."

Filled with his own sense of the moment, he said softly, "My pleasure, Ed. I'll see you in the shop." And he left.

He was gone, but he had left behind an aura of warmth and open-hearted generosity that worked a magic on the white, sterile room, as it had upon my sense of well-being. I was deeply moved by his loving-kindness, and sobered by the thought that I could not think of a single instance in which I had given of myself in the same way. But then I doubt that anyone would want to hazard an encounter with me wielding a straight-razor.

17

Every day, or two, a doctor would come and give the turnbuckle a twist or two, frequently followed by a radiologist who would take an X-ray of the progress. More than a month had passed when doctor Donato stopped by and told me that the sling arrangement had worked so well in repositioning my pelvis, they had decided that the slight variance did not justify further surgery to pin it together. He said the same was true regarding the compound fracture of my left leg; X-rays showed the break to be healing well enough to eliminate the need for further surgery.

He said my recovery to date was truly remarkable, and added, "It's only been five weeks, they are calling you our miracle case. So, we have decided to wrap you in a body cast and send you home."

I wasn't sure that I had heard him right. "Home?" I stammered, "you're sending me home? When?"

"Is tomorrow soon enough?"

For a long moment I was speechless; was I dreaming? Was this really happening? It was! "Yes! Oh, yes!" I shouted. "Thank you, doctor."

He placed his hand lightly on my shoulder, "You're welcome." He smiled, "There's a lot of healing yet to take place, keep up the good work." Then he turned and left.

I breathed, "*Thank you, God,*" and reached for the phone to tell Barbara the good news.

Early the next morning I was transported in my bed to the lower reaches of the hospital, to a large room that was a combination laboratory and physical therapy area. I have mentioned a number of times how fortunately, incredibly, pain-free I was during all the weeks I lay with my hips in a sling. That was about to change.

They unhooked the sling and stripped me of the hospital gown. Then lifting me up they positioned me stretched face-up on a piece of apparatus that surely came from the torture chambers of hell itself. My hips rested on a pedestal that felt no larger than a silver dollar, while my head and shoulders lay on the edge of a padded shelf.

Suspended between these two supports, it felt like the point of a spear was being driven into the base of my spine. The pain sent shock-waves of agony throughout my entire body. It was excruciating, beyond belief.

The pain continued unabated while two men, one on each side, swathed me in layer upon layer of saturated strips of plaster from my armpits to below my right knee. I was suspended between the pedestals so they could pass the plaster strips under my back and hips.

My left leg was already in a cast from my hip to my toes. To ensure that my pelvis was positioned correctly, and would remain so, they bent my right leg at the knee and cemented a plaster-covered board between it and my left knee immobilizing the entire area.

It seemed like they took forever but finally they were done, and the pain subsided. But then the cast reached so far up on my chest I felt like I couldn't take a full breath. That scared the hell out of me, and I complained. Their assurances that I could breathe did not satisfy me, and they finally cut a "v" in the top edge of the cast just under my chin. Then satisfied that the cast had hardened properly, they were joined by others and together moved me back to my bed. The intense pain still fresh in my mind I was glad to close my eyes and rest.

Sometime later they transported me by ambulance to my home where again, with extra help, they settled me in a specially equipped hospital bed that Barbara had ready. There I was, and there I would remain for the next seven weeks, like some misshapen turtle lying on its back. I felt like I had been dipped in concrete, and more immobilized than I had been in the hospital, for now I could move only my arms and my head. But I was happy, by God, happy to be home, and nothing could dampen the joy I felt.

I was released from the hospital the next day, a Saturday. The very next morning my son, Bryan, who was now almost three, climbed up into my bed and lay in the crook of my arm. Curious, he ran his hand over the surface of the cast.

"Does it hurt, Dad?"

"No, it doesn't, Bryan." I gave him a hug. "It feels just like a rock."

"Yes, it is like a rock. It protects my body while I get better."

"Want to watch T.V., Dad?"

"You bet." I clicked on the television and there was a preacher exhorting his congregation to change their sinful ways or they would spend an eternity in hell.

Bryan turned and looked at me, his blue eyes as clear, open and direct as a summer sky. He gazed at me for a long moment, then shook his head and said, "Not God, Dad. Not God!" I hugged him close and laid a kiss on the top of his head, and switched to a channel showing cartoons.

I didn't need a preacher to remind me, I was already in heaven.

18

Open and vulnerable in a way I had never before felt, time after time I found myself on the verge of tears. They were not tears of sadness or loss but of an unbearable feeling of love for everyone, and everything, and an inexpressible sense of joy at just being alive. And I realized that while wrapped like a mummy in a protective rock-hard casing, a far more impervious inner shell, a protective wall behind which I had lived for decades, lay in pieces.

My childhood vow, *I don't need you, I don't need anyone,* had long been an unconscious mantra in my life — and a conscious goal. The utter nonsense of that notion could no longer be denied. My weeks in the hospital were sufficient for even this stiff-necked, prideful fool to recognize the truth. But God, or my soul, was not finished with the lesson; I suspect they knew how easily I could forget.

To emphasize the point they chose a perfect metaphor, a plaster-cast shell within which I was even more confined, more dependent, on the love and care of others than I had been in the hospital. Peering out from that shell at the faces of those I loved, and who loved me, and at life bursting forth all around me, I was overcome with a love so intense that it hurt, and I cried for the wonder of it.

I was reminded of other times that spoke of my soul's hunger for such a love, brief, poignant episodes that had brought this hard-assed Marine and ex-cop to tears. Like the awakening, the epiphany, I had experienced in the simple beauty, and sacred silence, of that small wayside chapel in the Santa Cruz mountains on my first trip to California. There were others.

* * *

One evening while driving out to Thousand Oaks from the San Fernando Valley in the company car Tom had assigned to me, the sultry voice of Peggy Lee drifted out from the radio. It was her new release, Is That All There Is, *and I burst out laughing when I heard the lyrics.*

> *Is that all there is? Is that all there is?*
> *If that's all there is my friend,*
> *then let's keep dancing.*
> *Let's break out the booze,*
> *and have a ball,*
> *if that's all … there is.*

Is that all there is? The words seemed not to come so much from the radio as from some dark corner deep within me, a sad lament of chronic emptiness, an unappeased hunger for I knew not what. *And I laughed and laughed until tears filled my eyes.*

Then one morning a few days later, I sat in bed, a steaming cup of black coffee at my elbow, and read the opening lines of The Hound of Heaven, *that marvelous poem of God's pursuit of man, by Francis Thompson.*

The Hound of Heaven

I fled Him down the nights and down the days;
I fled Him down the arches of the years;
I fled Him down the labyrinthine ways of my own
mind, and in the mist of tears
I hid from Him under running laughter,
Up vistaed hopes I sped; and shot, precipitated,
Adown Titanic glooms of chasmed fears,
From those strong feet that followed,
Followed after.
But with unhurrying chase,
and unperturbed pace,
Deliberate speed, majestic instancy,
They beat — and a Voice beat
More instant than the Feet —
"All things betray thee, who betrayest Me."
(For though I knew His love who followed,
Yet was I sore adread
Lest having Him, I must have naught beside)

Unexpected tears blurred my vision, a sob caught in my throat, a flood of emotion washed over me — and I wept. The image of the poor creature who longed for God's love but feared the cost of embracing that love, was too close to my own soul's longing — and fear. The power and awful beauty of the words, the familiar images, the pounding rhythm of the chase and the flight, were like arrows of truth driven into my soul. Yet like him, I fled — weeping.

Never before had I considered these events, and my experience in the small chapel in the Santa Cruz mountains as being connected, and yet it was now obvious that they were. In each instance I had been caught unaware by the surfacing of a deep unconscious longing — my soul's hunger — a *blind quest*. How could I know that it would take a collision with a tree — a near-brush with death — for my eyes and my heart to be opened, like an oyster shell, to reveal the pearl of great price within?

19

The days took on a routine, as they had in the hospital, with one major difference; each day, each hour, was filled with, blessed by, an enveloping presence of love. Barbara could not have been more loving and attentive, and to be with and watch the irrepressible bundle of life that Bryan, our three-year-old son, brought to each day was a constant reminder of how incredibly fortunate and grateful I was to be alive. I could never thank God enough, though I tried mightily.

Convinced that the Intelligence and Energy of the One Divine Presence was at work in every cell of my body, I welcomed, embraced, the Holy Spirit — Wholeness. I was content to let it play out in its own perfect way and time.

After several weeks I was transported back to the hospital, to the room where they had wrapped my body in the full length cast. I lay on my back, as I had now for more than twelve weeks, and watched a young man wearing a protective mask over his nose and mouth approach me carrying what I soon realized was a surgical saw.

He clicked on the power and, beginning at a point just below my chin, began at once to cut through the cast. I could feel the action of the saw vibrating through my rib cage, and prayed that he knew where the cast ended and my skin began. He apparently did, for he quickly and efficiently cut the shell into pieces, removing everything but the cast on my left leg.

It was amazing, I felt weightless. Were it not for the cast on my leg to serve as an anchor, I might suddenly have floated right off the table. I wondered if this was how a butterfly felt when shed of its cocoon or a baby chick after pecking its way into the world. It was glorious, like being born again.

I looked down the length of my body. I had lost a lot of weight but everything looked — and felt — in good shape. I probably didn't weigh much more than I had when I graduated from the State Police Academy. But the attendants were not done with me yet.

They placed restraining straps over my chest and switched on a motor somewhere underneath the table; the end nearest my head began to lift. It had only risen about a foot when I told them I felt dizzy.

The motor clicked off and the attendant said, "That's your body adjusting to the change. Let me know when you feel okay, we'll take you up in gradual steps."

"Okay," I said. "I'm good."

They continued in this way until I was nearly upright, then paused while my body and my mind absorbed the change. It had been more than three months since I had had this view of my world, and had wondered if I ever would again. Yet here I was with the world settling back into its rightful place. I didn't know whether to laugh or cry.

They checked to see if I was feeling okay, then placed a parallel-bar assembly in front of me and helped me to stand between the bars, where I supported my weight on my right foot and extended arms. They asked me to take a step and I swung my right foot forward and planted my weight on it. It held; I could stand!

After weeks on my back wondering whether I would ever walk again, I had just taken my first step. They asked me to take two or three more, and I did. Tears of joy made it difficult for me to see; it was exhausting, but wonderful.

They smiled. "You did well," they said, then fitted me with crutches and showed me how to use them correctly. With their guidance, I soon got the hang of it.

"Okay," they said. "Just take it slow, don't overdo it." With that I was released and transported home. The cast on my left leg would remain for another five weeks, but I could walk! By God, I could walk!

20

I'll never forget the look of joy and relief on Barbara's face when I was helped from the ambulance and, with crutches tucked firmly under my armpits, I stood and took a step toward her. In an instant her arms were around my neck, her tear-streaked face buried in the hollow of my shoulder. I was still struggling with a lump in my own throat, when she leaned away and whispered, "Welcome back!"

I could only smile and nod as, together, we walked into the house. My eyes lit on the hospital bed in our family room, a stark reminder of where I had lain prisoner for the past seven weeks. "I'll be glad to get rid of that," I said.

"Are you sure you can climb the steps to the bedroom?"

"One way or another," I replied, "I intend to sleep in my own bed tonight," and hobbled into the family room and sat in *my* chair, a green leather lounge chair that faced the television and bore the imprint of my butt.

"Ah – h – h!" I sighed, "feels like home."

I heard the door to the patio glide open behind me and a joyful cry, "Daddy! Daddy!"

Bryan and our collie, Sean, came bounding into the room. I lifted Bryan into my lap and hugged him, and hugged him, while Sean pressed his soft muzzle under the crook of my arm. I rubbed him behind his ears and tugged at the soft, thick, white coat on his chest and, I swear, he too sighed with contentment and lay down.

Barbara watched all this, her eyes brimming with tears even as she laughed and clapped with joy. She placed a freshly brewed cup of coffee on a nearby tray-table and leaned over and kissed me. Giving me one of her direct looks she shook her head, "The doctors, I was so afraid, and here you are. Unbelievable. My God, we're lucky."

I looked at her for a long moment, then at Bryan, and at Sean, "We certainly are, Babe."

Evening came and I stood at the bottom of the stairs leading up to our bedroom. It seemed longer and higher than I remembered, each step a huge challenge. The brief training I received for walking with crutches had not included negotiating stairs, and I hadn't used them enough to feel all that confident. I damned well did not want to fall. Then another possibility occurred to me.

I turned around and sat down on the stairs, handed the crutches to Barbara, and placing my hands on the step behind me lifted my body up step-by-step backwards until I reached the top.

I had a silly grin on my face as Barbara helped me to my feet; she just shook her head. Whether that was in response to my creative locomotion, or concern with the fact that my hips had taken the brunt of the journey, I never asked. But I slept in my own bed that night — and every night thereafter. The next day I learned that by using only one crutch, and the stair rail, I could now easily climb or descend any flight of stairs.

A few weeks later I returned once more to the hospital, where they removed the cast from my leg. I looked at my leg with the same curiosity I might have had if it belonged to someone else; I hadn't seen it for many weeks. It was thinner than I remembered but then, so was my entire body. It troubled me to discover that I couldn't bend my knee, but the attendant told me to not worry about it, that time and physical therapy would restore full movement.

As it turned out we had our own solution for physical therapy. During the weeks I lay in the body cast, we had a pool and Jacuzzi built in our back yard. Two or three times a day I would slip into the stimulating hot waters to work my left leg, often followed by a stint in the pool. The 103 degree churning waters worked their magic and brought a steady increase of movement in my knee joint. At first I worked it with my left foot planted on the floor or against the opposite wall, and the flexing was slight. But soon after achieving some initial movement, I started doing squats and steadily increased the flexion until I was able to do full deep-knee bends.

It took far less time than I anticipated, and soon enough I was good as new — almost. My left leg was a tad shorter than my right, but that was negligible considering the massive assault my body had suffered, and the swiftness with which it recovered.

Amazingly, unbelievably, I was back! After only five weeks in the hospital, not the predicted eighteen months, and seven weeks in a body cast, full recovery was in sight. And contrary to the doctor's predictions, there were no follow-on surgeries. It was nothing short of a miracle.

21

The Jacuzzi and pool not only provided the necessary elements for working the physical kinks out of my body, but proved to be a perfect spot for meditation and reflection on the total experience. I felt changed at some basic level, for the better I hoped, and longed to understand it, assimilate it — embrace it.

I was sitting in the Jacuzzi with my eyes closed, my arms splayed out along the lip of the deck, while one of the powerful jet streams pummeled my lower back, when I heard the door to our family room open.

When I opened my eyes and saw it was my friend Neil who stepped out on the patio deck, I smiled and shouted, "Just the guy I wanted to see."

He ducked and turned away as though he had stepped onto the wrong patio. Laughing at his antic, I shouted, "Hey, get your butt over here. We need to talk."

He grinned, ambled over, and pulled up a deck chair. "You certainly seem to be in good spirits."

I spread my arms expansively "How could I not be?" and added, "I'll be back at work part-time beginning next week."

"You're kidding," he said. "What's next? Are you going to buy that Yamaha?"

"No, my cycle-riding days are over; I want to be around to watch Bryan grow up."

"That sounds like a wise choice, what else have you learned these past months?"

"More, it seems, than I can wrap my mind around. I was just grappling with that very thing before you came through the door. It feels like it was an initiation of some kind, a rebirth, an awakening."

"To tell the truth, I look in the mirror and see a familiar face and body, but my heart tells me a different story. It's like that old television series in which three different people would claim to be Joe Blow. At the end of the program the moderator would say, 'Will the *real* Joe Blow please stand up.' I feel like I'm waiting for the a*nnouncer* to say, 'Will the *real* Ed Tuttle please stand up.

"Barbara, with her quirky sense of humor, says that I'm a 'walk-in,' that some wandering soul saw me cash in my chips, and decided it was a great opportunity for another go-round."

Neil chuckled and said, "Well, buddy, I don't know about that, but I've noticed a gentleness about you that I never saw before, less of the hard-assed ex-marine and state police sergeant."

"Yeah, I know, and that's part of it. I feel so full of love and gratitude, so blessed at just being alive; it's overwhelming."

Neil just nodded in response, and we sat quiet for a time, each caught up in his own thoughts. I broke the silence with a question. "Do you remember when we first met we discussed which is better; to *believe*, or to *know*?"

"I'll never forget it. I think you had already staked out *to know*. If it was a choice today, I too would choose *to know*, but the query was flawed for the two are not separate, they are part of a single process. We first *believe*, start with a premise. If that belief is strong enough, important enough, we act on it and get a result. It's the way in which we get to *know* anything. "There is an old Chinese saying:

"What I hear, I forget. What I see, I remember. What I do, I understand" — *know!*

Neil was quiet for a moment, as though considering my torrent of words, then a grin creased his face. "I believe," he said. "No, I *know,* you'll find what it is you seek."

I laughed. "Thanks, pal. I can always count on you."

He stood up, clapped me on the shoulder and said, "Now, that's something you *do* know." He had his hand on the patio door when, with a laugh, I shouted, "I *believe* it!" He shook his head, gave a final wave, and was gone.

22

I stood up and stepped from the spa into the pool. A thrill rippled up my spine as I dropped quickly into the 75-degree water and struck out for the opposite end of the pool. After a half-dozen lazy laps I rolled over on my back, closed my eyes, and surrendered to the natural buoyancy of the water, while my mind drifted free. Relieved of conscious effort and clamor, it brought to light some things that I now clearly *knew*, which I previously only *believed*.

I *knew*, without the slightest doubt, my years of study and practice of the principles of the Science of Mind was a primary factor in the swiftness and completeness with which I healed.

I was *convinced* that the mind which we call *our* mind is an extension — a replica — of the One Mind; "made in It's image and likeness." It is similar to the relation of an off-site terminal to an immense server computer or, even more intimately, and accurately — like a son to a father.

I *knew* it was my task to be aware of that, and to make sure I was *connected* and *turned-on*. This I did by prayer, meditation, and affirmations sprinkled liberally throughout the days and nights, something I constantly reinforced by seeing everyone and everything that touched my life in any way as the perfect activity of the One.

Long before the accident I was aware of the incredible creative power of a mind focused on, and convinced of, a desired outcome. It had proven to be the case in so many ways prior to the accident: as increased abundance, loving relationships, satisfying and challenging employment and much more.

And the *Vision* I had in Intensive Care blessed me with a clear and convincing sense of the Unity of all — of a Wholeness — which is the essential nature of God. No one is left out, nor are we separate from each other, or from the natural world.

Like many, I had wondered if there is life *out there*, beyond the range of our limited vision, as though we are the exception. Truth is, there is nothing but Life, out there, in here — everywhere God is — and nothing else.

I *knew* I could have died lying next to that shiny new motorcycle on a lonely stretch of blacktop, with the sun shining down upon me. But I didn't. So, with all that I knew — or thought I knew — there remained the mystery.

It is not surprising that God works in mysterious ways his wonders to perform; it is, however, a humbling experience to be the recipient, and wonder why.

I had received a precious gift, one to rival

the Holy Grail, had been touched as though by the hand of God. It filled me with the certainty that within each of us there *is* that Presence — *that Intelligence and Energy* — which is forever revealing It's Self as God's healing love, power, and grace.

Then my eyes flew open as a startling question played across my mind. Was all of this just about *my* personal awakening, the correcting of a self-centered attitude toward life that led to the life-threatening collision with a tree? Or was it some deep, unfulfilled hunger of my soul on its journey back to union with God?

My soul had a mind of its own, a vision and a longing that covered many lifetimes. It could be that for my soul the "accident" was no accident, but a timely and effective way of opening my eyes, and my mind, to a greater vision of life and of God.

If that's the case, my soul and I will enthusiastically continue our joint quest toward that ultimate union with the One, the Author of all life.

I found I had drifted to the pool steps. Sitting on one I leaned back, my face lifted to the afternoon sun and thought, *it doesn't get any better than this* and then — it did!

Bryan, in bright yellow swim trunks, came running from the house, and leaped into my waiting arms.

Ed Tuttle brings a unique blend of eastern and western spiritual thought to his life and his writing. A retired minister, he is the author of two previous works: **Sacred Stories Sacred Dreams: Bible Myth and Metaphor**, a mythic view of biblical stories, and **Raindrops in the Dust: Dreams, Memories, and Reflections**, a collection of essays, poems, and dreamy musings woven together into what one reviewer described as *"a unique species of spiritual autobiography."*